Pump it up

Christmas 2018 Edition - Vol. 3 - Issue # 10

I0339196

Mitchell Coleman Jr.
Bringing Home The Funk!

FASHION DOLLS
The Next Hot Fashion Accessory

Merry Christmas!

Beauty
5 essential anti-ageing rules

Writing & Placing Christmas & Holiday Songs

TOP TIPS

* Best Gifts Ideas For Music Lovers
* Treat Yourself at the 10 Best Spas in Los Angeles

Movies
NETFLIX Christmas must watch

HUMANITARIAN AWARENESS - California fires: How to help victims of Woolsey Fire

Enjoy The Sound Of
Pump it up
RADIO

Get the free Pump it up magazine Radio App on your smartphone or tablet, and you'll never miss your favourite music!

POP - ROCK - DANCE - RNB - JAZZ
Available on Google Play Store
www.**PumpItUpMagazine**.com

PUMP IT UP MAGAZINE
LINKS

WEBSITE
www.pumpitupmagazine.com

FACEBOOK
www.facebook.com/pumpitupmagazine

TWITTER
www.twitter.com/pumpitupmag

SOUNDCLOUD
www.soundcloud.com/pumpitupmagazine

INSTAGRAM
pumpitupmagazine

PINTEREST
www.pinterest.com/pumpitupmagazine

PUMP IT UP MAGAZINE
30721 Russell Ranch Road
Suite 140
Westlake Village,
California 91362
United States
www.pumpitupmagazine.com
info@pumpitupmagazine.com
Tel : (001) (877)841 – 7414 (toll free number)

EDITORIAL

CONTRIBUTORS

EDITOR IN CHIEF
Anissa Boudjaoui

FASHION EDITOR
Carol Mongo

MUSIC EDITOR
Michael B. Sutton
Scott Galloway

STYLE CORRECTOR
Olivia Ferel

PARTNERS

Phase Global Radio

Delit Face

The Sound Of L.A.

L.A. Unlimited

Editions L.A.

Merry Christmas Everyone!

As the year 2018 comes to a close and I reflect back, I am truly grateful and blessed in more ways than one can imagine.

This year had many great reviews and interviews by some wonderful and talented independent artists.

For 2019 we have a few surprises in the coming issues that we hope will pique your interest and keep you smiling and enjoying Pump It Up Magazine!

Have a safe, blessed and joyous holiday!

Peace and Blessings!

Anissa Boudjaoul
Founder

Pump it up Magazine

TABLE OF CONTENTS

EDITORIAL
Page 3

6

MITCHELL COLEMAN JR.
Bringing Home The Funk!

FASHION DOLLS
The Next Hot Fashion Accessory

10

IN THE SPOTLIGHT
Music : Aneessa "Back To Life"
Michael B. Sutton "T.S.O.L.A."
Book : Michel Jordi "Ignite That Spark"

BEAUTY
5 essential anti-ageing rules

MERRY CHRISTMAS
- Best Gifts Ideas For Music Lovers
- Treat Your Loved Ones At One Of The Best Spas In L.A.

20

26

MOVIES
Netflix Christmas Movies

TOP TIPS
Writing and Placing Christmas and Holidays Songs

HUMANITARIAN AWARENESS
How To Help The Victims Of Woolsey Fires

Pump it up
MAGAZINE

MITCHELL COLEMAN JR. IS BRINGING THE FUNK HOME!

Music veteran Mitchell Coleman Jr. has made many strides in his blossoming career as a bass player and composer. Often noted for his contributions in the arena of jazz-funk fusion and collaborations with some great musicians including keyboardist Herman "Hollywood" Jenkins, Mitchell has built an impressive catalog of music. Mitchell's current work with producer Michael B Sutton is equally phenomenal as evident from his upcoming single Twilight.

WHO ARE YOU, AND WHAT DO YOU DO?
My name is Mitchell Coleman Jr, and I am an electric bass player.

WHO ARE YOUR PRIMARY MUSICAL INFLUENCES? AT THE TIME I STARTED PLAYING BASS, I WAS GREATLY INFLUENCED BY MARK ADAMS FROM THE FUNK GROUP SLAVE. IN THE BEGINNING, MY MUSICAL APPROACH COULD BE DEFINED AS "UNFILTERED, TAKE NO PRISONERS FUNK".
As I developed, I really got into Marcus Miller – especially after hearing his work on David Sanborn's, "Straight to the Heart" (1984). I started to hear the music that touched me. I did not have the ear for heavy jazz, and did not know how to approach it. But then there was the collaboration between Miles Davis and Marcus Miller and the gap between jazz, and the funk I enjoy, was bridged and I started to hear a sophistication I did not hear before! Later, I got into Larry Graham (the father of the thump), Stanley Clarke, and Jaco Pastorius messed up all my barely-developed musical theory. Those days confirmed to me that although the musicians I mentioned are great, and can be used as wonderful references… You can only be who you are, and you have to find your own voice.

"You can only be who you are, and you have to find your own voice."

WHAT ARE YOU LISTENING TO MUSICALLY, IN THE PAST 12 MONTHS THAT HAS ENHANCED THE WAY YOU THINK ABOUT MUSIC AND YOUR CRAFT?
listening to Miles Davis, Joe Zawinul and Steely Dan.
I love the way these great musicians can take something seemingly "straight head", and take it (musically) sideways creating mood changes and taking listeners on a magical musical journey.

HOW DOES YOUR PERSONAL MUSICAL VOICE DIRECTLY RELATE TO THE FUNCTION OF THE BASSES? ALSO, WHAT ARE YOUR MAIN INSTRUMENTS?
I approach each musical situation like a conversation. Like any conversation I am having, there is a time that I will speak and express my thoughts and emotions… depending on the subject. While others are speaking, I am listening, showing interest and providing support.

5. HOW DOES MUSIC AFFECT YOUR CULTURE AND IMMEDIATE ENVIRONMENT?
Growing up as a product of divorced parents… I was alone a lot of the time. So, music became a comforter and friend to me. But, being alone also allowed me to discover and developed my own musical voice.

DESCRIBE YOUR STANDING PRACTICE REGIMEN. ALSO, WHAT TECHNICAL (AND MUSICAL) ASPECTS OF YOUR PLAYING ARE YOU CURRENTLY WORKING ON?
I started off playing everything that appealed to me as a bass player. Later, I would try to play the things that did not appeal to me. Naturally, I learned the songs that appealed to me faster! But, I learned more from the ones that did not.
I try to play something new every day by ear and then work on reading. Scales are also great for reference, and I am really getting into modes now – which seem to be the gatekeepers to the mood changes I love so much.

HOW IMPORTANT IS IT TO UNDERSTAND THE LANGUAGE OF MUSIC?
Like any language, music allows communication. In order to communicate well… you must have something to say. More importantly… you need to listen to what is being said.

WHAT ADVICE WOULD YOU GIVE TO A YOUNG, UP AND COMING BASS PLAYER?
Practice, Practice Practice!

 Mitchellcolemanjrofficialfanpage
 MitchOnTheBass
 mitchellcolemanjr.com

MITCHELL COLEMAN JR.
is bringing serious heat with this funky thumping bass track!
Twilight
Latest single from the smash album
GRAVITY
Available Nov. 9th, 2018

Fashion Dolls

Fashionistas, listen up!

The next hot fashion accessory will be neither a logo emblazoned handbag nor a fancy pair of stilettos or even an armful of shiny bracelets.

On the contrary, it will be a fashion doll!
Let me tell you why.

When iconic couturier, Karl Lagerfeld poses next to a 12 inch figurine he's just dressed for a publicity shot, it's a signal that dolls are no longer child's play. It's serious business for both the designer and the collector!

Collaborations between major doll makers and international fashion giants: **Louis Vuitton, Burberry, Zuhair Murad, Herve Leger, and Montaigne Market,** further underscore the credibility and importance high fashion lends to today's collector doll.

So after indulging in designer jeans, designer bags and designer smart phone covers, is it all that crazy to give into the designer dressed fashion doll as a new way to express your taste in style!

Though Barbie--once the only best dressed doll on the planet-- usually serves as the gateway into collecting, she is not the only vinyl diva on the block. There is a plethora of dolls on the market today. Moreover, the internet is awash with specialized blogs, online stores and community forums (like this one), each chocked with a wealth of information on doll "families" of varying sizes, shapes, looks, ethnicities and price points. Choosing a doll is as easy as…well…buying a pair of shoes. We like a particular doll not only because she's pretty and svelte, but also because she's got the kind of swag we connect with. And just as you do for yourself, you can always change her look by painting on a new shade of lipstick, smoothing back her hair, and of course, dressing dolly to reflect the latest fashion trends or celebrity whelms.

Whether you purchase dolly's clothes or design them yourself, you are the master of her world much in the way a Hollywood pro takes control over a celebrity for her red carpet events. You become the stylist, maybe even the fashion designer. And since you will ultimately post your pics on social media, Add photographer and possibly (blog) editor to this virtual resume.

Nikes or Jimmy Choos, Juicy Couture or Dior, boxers or briefs….anything you that makes you drool can be duplicated in miniature.

The fashion doll, after all, reflects the fashionista that we are, the style maven we were, or the drop dead gorgeous diva we aspire to be.

Our closets may be limited to jeans, t-shirts and other mundane basics, but the fashions of our dreams are fueled by the beautiful people who walk the red carpet events, romp down the catwalks and peer out from the glossy pages of tabloid magazines.

Their sexy dresses, edgy footwear, baubles, beads and lipstick make us fantasize about participating in such a glamorous world.

And while we may not have the funds, opportunity or the lifestyle to support such pricey items for ourselves, anything is possible and everything becomes accessible (if not affordable) when shrunk down to the Lilliputian proportions.

The pleasure of owning a piece designer fashion, even in doll form, remains just as thrilling!

Looking for more information about collector dolls? Here are three very popular doll blogs to get you started:

insidethefashiondollstudio.com
Information and lots of photos of collector dolls.

blackdollcollecting.blogspot.com
Debby Garrette's very large, historical and diverse collection of black dolls. Interesting stories!

fashiondollstylist.blogspot.com
Once you get a doll, learn how to keep her in the height of high fashion. Lots of tutorials, lots of ideas and the latest fashion news from catwalks and red carpets translated into doll fashion.

By the way, these collector dolls aren't sold in local stores. You can do a search for "Fashion Royalty" or "Barbie Model Muse" on eBay or consult their websites:

https://barbie.mattel.com
Barbie's official website. Search: "Signature" for dolls destined for adult collectors.

https://integritytoys.com
The official website of Integrity Toys' Fashion Royalty dolls. They don't sell much on their site but they offer a list of online retailers.

Photos : Courtesy Fashion Doll Stylist

Written by Carol Mongo.

ANEESSA
"BACK TO LIFE"

FRENCH DANCE MUSIC STAR ANEESSA (FORMERLY LADY ANEESSA) MAKES AMERICAN DEBUT WITH SULTRY MODERN COVER OF SOUL II SOUL'S "BACK TO LIFE"

Dance music fans in Europe and abroad are intimately familiar with superstar Aneessa from her international club hits "Jamais," "Us," "Dance with Me," "Sur Mes Terres," "I Can't Let You Go" and "It's on You."

Her album Ce soir racked up two-million streams in Asia alone. Now after a 3-year hiatus, Lady Aneessa has reinvented herself as just Aneessa now and is making her bold U.S. debut with a sexy cover of "Back to Life," the game-changing dance classic created by the group Soul II Soul back in 1989.

Produced, arranged by Michael B. Sutton (former Motown writer/producer of Marvin Gaye, Michael Jackson, Dennis Edwards and more), the smooth and sensual groove is an instant attention-getter which matches perfectly with everything Aneessa is bringing stateside from abroad.

Aneessa is looking forward to introducing herself to American audiences and beyond via a series of more intimate shows than she has ever put on in the past. She is targeting a spring 2019 release for her next album (as yet untitled), likely to be preceded by one more single or two.

Back to Life' is the perfect statement for me at this time," Aneessa declares. *"It fits with my life – I'm a `90s girl! New styles such as Reggaeton were big back then and I am loving redoing this song in my own style: smooth and sultry."*

"Also, so much is new in my life," Aneessa continues. "new life, new country, new romance. I recorded my fourth and last album R&B in French in 2015 then performed my last shows as Lady Aneessa in Italy and Paris.

The French have a different mentality about art, especially music; they don't consider it a real job.

IN THE SPOTLIGHT

"BACK TO LIFE" (Single)
Aneessa

Aneessa comes across as spiritual and emotional immersing herself in her music with a soulful heart even more adventurous and pushing herself in occasionally new directions to give listeners a different sound.
Available Now Everywhere !

To know more about Aneessa, please vist her website:
www.aneessa.com

T.S.O.L.A. (THE SOUND OF LOS ANGELES) - Single
Michael B. Sutton

The maestro of smooth grooves Michael B. Sutton returns with yet another delightful offering upon the release of his new single T.S.O.L.A. (The Sound Of L.A.). Sutton is often noted for his work with Motown Records and has consistently remained active as an artist and producer in recent years. In fact, T.S.O.L.A. is the second single Sutton has released in less than three months, the first being Sex U, which came out this past September.
T.S.O.L.A. has an enchanting vibe. The track draws its sonic landscape from elements of both r&b and contemporary jazz. T.S.O.L.A. opens with the well-orchestrated sounds of synth strings and a driving beat before breaking into its intoxicating bassline and layered brass instruments that add much to this composition's depth. Available Now Everywhere!

IGNITE THAT SPARK (BOOK)
Michel Jordi

To be an entrepreneur is to break free and to live your passion Disrupting the traditional way we look at business through imagery and music is the purpose of this captivating and unique handbook. This has been my inspiration to approach life, freedom, work and the making of the business plan.
"Swiss Ethno Pope" Michel Jordi has been known since the 1990s for his Swiss Ethno Fever products, which brought him international fame and recognition. In November 2017, he published his autobiography "GUTS– Giving Up is No Option" in German. On November 19th, 2018, he launched his new book "Ignite That Spark – 10 Commandments of Entrepreneurship" at University College London (UCL). True to his reputation as a serial disrupter, he has opted to follow that path by linking the book with a pop song. However, it is not "just another song," but instead a strong and encouraging message for up-and-coming generations. The lyrics reflect Michel Jordi's life and were written by Franceska Aeschlimann. The music was composed by British singer-songwriter Chris Eaton who performs it in a duet with Abby Eaton. Jordi's time is now dedicated to inspire and advise aspiring entrepreneurs to realize their own dreams.

More information is available on our webpage
www.ignitethatspark.com

EDITIONS L.A.

GRAPHIC AND WEB **DESIGN**

WEBSITE
CD COVER
LOGO
FLYER
BANNERS
EPK
LYRICS VIDEO
TRANSLATION

We give you the tools to make your song or band to be heard around the world !

**INFO@
EDITIONS-L.A.COM**

WWW.EDITIONS-LA.COM

SPECIAL OFFERS 50% ON LYRICS VIDEOS
HIGH-QUALITY MUSIC LYRICS VIDEO
UP TO 1080P HD VIDEO QUALITY
MODERN AND SIMPLE STYLE
$250 FOR MUSIC VIDEO UP TO 4 MIN
$350 FOR MUSIC VIDEO UP TO 5 MIN

FOR MORE INFO VISIT WWW.EDITIONS-LA.COM

Just in time to add a log onto fall evening fires, renowned former Motown songwriter/producer Michael B. Sutton is flexing his trademark sense for sensuality on his first single as a recording artist in 15 years, "Sex U." Released via his own Little Dizzy Records company via Sound of L.A. Records (a distribution company for which he is also its CEO), "Sex U" is a remix of the song "I Wanna Sex You" which Michael first recorded on his collector's item CD Hopeless Romantic back in 2003. "Sex U" is the lead single from his long-awaited follow-up album (as yet untitled) that Michael kept putting off due to all of the other artists he has been producing and projects he has been overseeing as a multi-hyphenated executive, including new music by his wife, Aneessa (a fiery update of Soul II Soul's "Back to Life") and his daughter Dionyza ("If it Kills"). Michael is ecstatic to return to his first love of singing songs of love, lust and romance for fans that like their music on the soulful spicy side.

Michael says of "Sex U," "It's about feeling sexy more than having sex.
My intention is for couples to elevate their thinking to not put so much emphasis on sex as opposed to sexuality as a spiritual thing. The best sex is deep and beautiful - a God-given journey of emotion and physicality for us to explore with gusto and passion. Lovers should see themselves like ice cream - free to lick and lap on each other as they please! While some may shy away from it, there is a very sexual aspect to romance that should never be ignored nor separated from love. Courtship, seduction, consummation – they all go together hand in hand…torso to torso."

"Sex U" is a torrid collaboration between Michael B. Sutton and co-remixer Christian B. that includes new guitar parts by session/touring A-lister Tommy Organ ("Michael Jackson's This Is It" and "The George Lopez Show"), sizzling percussion by Timbali and background vocals by Dioynza.

The release of "Sex U" is poignant for Michael as that is the month his new wife Aneessa came from Paris to join him in Los Angeles one year ago, thus inspiring an intimate new batch of songs that will fill his upcoming masterwork – bridging his provocative to a divinely soaring future ahead. "We're soulmates from different backgrounds, Michael concludes. "Her presence in my life wrote these songs into my heart and I sang them back to her with words of love."

Order Michael B Sutton " Sex U" today!
Amazon: https://amzn.to/2MTgp5X
iTunes: https://apple.co/2pBTKC1

DELIT FACE

Social Media For The Entertainment World
MUSIC & MOVIE Industry

SINGER
SONGWRITER
MUSICIANS
PRODUCERS
PUBLISHERS
DISTRIBUTORS
MUSIC SUPERVISORS

ACTORS
DIRECTORS
PRODUCERS
DISTRIBUTORS
SET DESIGNERS
SCRIPT WRITERS
EXTRAS

MAKE UP ARTISTS
HAIR STYLISTS
PHOTOGRAPHERS
GRAPHIC DESIGNER

Register now FREE and connect with people in your industry
www.delitface.com

BEST GIFTS IDEAS FOR MUSIC LOVERS

No-Fail Gifts Ideas for Music Lovers
The perfect gifts for music lovers are the ones that help them enjoy music even more, or show off their love of music. These gifts are designed to do just that and are some of the best music gifts you can give.

WIRELESS SHOWER SPEAKER

For those that don't want to go 10 minutes without their music, get them this wireless shower speaker, and they'll be able to sing their way through the shower. It's also a good way to listen to your favorite morning radio show in the shower. $50

BOSE ACOUSTIC NOISE CANCELLING HEADPHONES

These noise cancelling headphones are amazing. They'll drown out all of the background noise and bring the music the way it should be heard. Works great on a plane, and also in a room that is quiet, since it makes it even more quiet. $270

LEARN TO PLAY PIANO DVDS

For those that have always wanted to play piano, but never got up the gumption to take lessons, these DVDs will do the job of an instructor. They'll be playing simple songs in no time, and be able to move on to bigger songs as they progress. $100

PORTABLE TURNTABLE

This turntable goes where they go so they can always have their music with them. It not only plays vinyl records, it plays MP3s, so it does a good job of covering decades of musical technology in one device. $99

A STREAMING SUBSCRIPTION

Just 10 years ago, if you wanted to buy someone music for Christmas, you'd probably have picked up an iTunes gift card (or even physical media). These days we're used to subscription-based streaming technology from the likes of Spotify, Pandora, and the relative newcomer, Apple Music instead.

Spotify sells $30 gift cards which provide enough credit for three months' use in the U.S. store. Pandora also offers a one-year subscription to Pandora Plus.

One of the most important things to determine when looking at purchasing a subscription is which service the recipient is using, or at least has access to. There's little point in buying someone a Spotify membership if they've built up an Apple Music library and they're happy with the service — so do some research first.

THE IMMERSIVE AUDIOPHILE POD

Now that we have your attention, we know it's unlikely that you'll drop $32k to give someone the gift of music, but we just had to show you this. It's been optimized for perfect acoustics so you are hearing the music exactly how it was intended to be heard. $32000

IPOD TABLE TOP JUKEBOX

This jukebox doesn't need nickels, quarters, or dollars, it connects to your iPod and plays your playlist with the press of a button. Really cool gift for music lovers that are something to do with that old iPod of theirs. $235

BOSE WAVE SOUNDTOUCH MUSIC SYSTEM

The Bose Wave system is one that you have to listen to in order to fully appreciate what it can do. The crisp, clear sound it produces is perfect for those that really get into their music and want to hear it the best way possible. $600

PERSONALIZED MIXTAPE DOORMAT

This doormat is personalized so that you can put the name of the family on it. It resembles an old school mixtape and is perfect for those that still listen to a ton of music from back in the day. The personalization makes it extra special and something they'll actually use. $38

TREAT YOUR LOVED ONE AT ONE OF THE BEST HOTEL SPAS IN L.A. !

Take your trip to the next level with a luxurious, pampering treatment at one of L.A.'s best hotel spas.

For weeks now, you've talked about treating yourself to a nice deep-tissue massage. And the idea of a scented steam bath, followed by a manicure and maybe even a facial (why not?) doesn't sound so bad either. Call it a staycation, call it a mental health day.

However you want to rationalize your visit to one of L.A.'s heavenly hotel spas is fine with us. From luscious coffee-and-lemon body scrubs to Chinese acupuncture or mineral soaking pools, each of these hotel spas offers a slightly different twist on "aahhh." And we guarantee you'll be impressed with the results.

SLS HOTEL
Central LA

The ultra-modern (and ultra-pricey), SLS Beverly Hills is a design dream where visual stimulation and lots of luxury abound. Aside from the ultra-modern décor, two restaurants, and complimentary BMW house cars, SLS also boasts Ciel Spa, a 5,000-square-foot sanctuary, where freshly-squeezed agua fresca will be waiting for you as you enter the long, Philippe Starck-designed hallway.
Every detail has been considered here, and treatments are customized for anything you may need; relaxing masage, healing body work, lymphatic drainage, slimming and tightening wraps, on and on.

Never thought you could fall asleep to a facial? Try one here and you'll be pleasantly surprised.

SHUTTERS ON THE BEACH
Santa Monica

Formerly a cool retreat for hot Hollywood stars and now a sister to Casa del Mar, Shutters has a relaxed but decidedly upscale style. And the freestanding One Spa is so close to the ocean, you can almost feel your toes in the sand as you begin to unwind. Enter the nautical-themed retreat—you'll feel as though you've walked onto a boat or a swank yacht—where the understated sophistication (a lá wainscoting galore) keeps in theme with the hotel's Cape Cod style.

Our favorite treatment is the Hammam Detoxifying Retreat, which starts with a coffee and lemon scrub followed by a clay wrap, Vichy shower and heated, deep-tissue massage. Emblematic of the the hotel's relaxed, beach-forward style is the gorgeous, comfy spa lounge—a dimly-lit, votive-filled living room-like space decked out in seashells.

BEVERLY WILSHIRE
Beverly Hills

The ornate detailing on this Four Seasons-operated gem, famous for its role in Pretty Woman, recalls 19th-century French splendor, but recent additions like Cut and the Blvd add 21st-century sophistication. The semi-hidden spa, located in the hotel's south tower, is worth a peek: Head to the twinkling steamroom, where light therapy is used from the ceiling and a crystal geode provides soothing energy to the room. Rinse off

with an ice cold rn shower, choose one of three settings: Caribbean rain, Atlantic storm and cold mist—and then head to the relaxation room for tea, fruit, nuts and house-made dark chocolate. This is Rodeo Drive, after all, so treatments like the diamond facial and the diamond magnetic are in-demand—therapists use dust made from real crushed diamonds to eliminate dry skin (a head-to-toe massage follows). Above all, the staff is gracious and the treatment rooms are blissful; though the crowd is wealthy and occasionally stuffy, there's still something warm about the place.

TERRANEA
Rancho Palos Verdes/Rolling Hills Estates

Situated on an oceanside bluff in posh Rancho Palos Verdes, the picturesque 102-acre resort is a aecca of relaxation and resort life. The sprawling 50,000-square-foot spa boasts a boutique, pool, cafe and gym, with free fitness classes. Open-air spin, anyone? But it's the oceanfront terrace we just can't stop dreaming about: After being invigorated with a Honey Body Bliss body scrub (which uses honey from the resort's own bee hives), you'll emerge onto a sun-drenched balcony with straight-on views of the glittering Pacific. The soundtrack to your session will waft in on a salty breeze. We can't imagine you'll want to leave the spa afterward, so relax in one of the lounges for the rest of the day.

5 ESSENTIALS
ANTI AGEING RULES

TO KEEP YOUR SKIN LOOKING

YOUNG

FRESH

GLOWING

AND PLUMP!

RULE ONE: EAT YOURSELF YOUNG
ADD THESE AGE-DEFYING SUPERFOODS TO YOUR WEEKLY SHOP AND TAKE YEARS OFF WITH EVERY BITE!

AVOCADOS are high in vitamin E and skin-protecting antioxidants. They also have a high folate content, which helps skin cell regeneration, giving you a more youthful complexion.
BLUEBERRIES are rich in vitamin C, which boosts blood circulation and helps your body produce collagen to keep your skin looking plump and healthy. It's also packed with potassium, which combats puffiness.
OILY FISH like salmon, sardines and mackerel are full of omega-3 fatty acids, which help beat dehydration, keeping skin looking dewy. These essential fats also help your body produce a layer on the top of the skin to seal in moisture.
BROCCOLI contains sulforaphane, which helps boost skin cells and clear toxins that can lead to fine lines.
RED CABBAGE is a winning source of phytonutrients that help slow the formation of wrinkles and hyperpigmentation.
MELON is stuffed with carotenoids, which stimulate the production of vitamin A. Vitamin A protects your skin from oxidative stress, slowing the ageing process.

RULE TWO: TAKE SKIN-FRIENDLY SUPPLEMENTS
EATING SKIN-PERFECTING FOODS IS ESSENTIAL, BUT THESE SUPPLEMENTS WILL SUPERCHARGE AGE-DEFYING RESULTS.
LYCOPENE: Derived from the humble tomato, lycopene helps protect your skin from UV ray damage one of the biggest causes of premature aging.
OMEGA-3S: Taking a supplement stuffed with these good fats will help your skin cells create a barrier to harmful toxins, but let skin-boosting nutrients in for moister, softer and suppler skin.
Collagen makes up around 75 per cent of your body's skin tissue, so when it's depleted you lose that firm, springy look and get wrinkles. The level of collagen in your skin drops by 1.5 per cent a year after the age of 25, so it's best to start topping it up as early on as you can.
CO-ENZYME Q10 keeps skin cells working efficiently. The antioxidants help beat sun damage, stimulate skin cell activity and collagen production and fight damage caused by pollution, toxins and stress.
GREEN TEA EXTRACT is pumped full of potent antioxidants, revitalising skin and flushing out toxins that lead to fine lines.

RULE THREE: AGE-PROOF YOUR SKINCARE REGIME
The way you treat your skin first thing in the morning and last thing at night has a major impact on how youthful and dewy it looks. Here are some proven ways to lock in moisture and keep fine lines at bay.
DON'T OVER-CLEANSE: It strips your skin of natural oils, leaving it dry and inflamed. Instead, rub a gentle, fragrance-free cleanser that contains antioxidants into your skin in circular motions to increase blood flow and remove make-up.
DON'T SKIP THE SERUM: Use it before you moisturise. Serums are thinner than moisturisers and their ingredients are more concentrated so they sink deep into your skin.
PROTECT THROUGH THE DAY: Your daytime moisturiser should contain sun protection with an SPF of at least 30 all year round and should protect against both UVA and UVB to limit sun damage.
CLEANSE THOROUGHLY AT NIGHT: Take your time over it so your skin is ready to fully absorb the nutrients in your night cream.
REPAIR AS YOU SLEEP: Your skin renews itself overnight. Help the process along with active creams containing plumping peptides, anti-ageing retinol and toxin-beating antioxidants. Massage using upwards and outward strokes to give skin a lift.
ALWAYS USE AN EYE CREAM: Eyes are the first area to wrinkle, so use one that contains SPF for the day, and a 'repairing' one at night. Apply after cleanser and serum with your ring finger, working from the inside out very gently.

RULE FOUR: KNOW YOUR AGE-DEFYING INGREDIENTS
Look out for these ingredients on your favourite beauty products and rest assure they'll keep your skin looking youthful!

WRITING AND PLACING CHRISTMAS AND HOLIDAY SONGS FOR MOVIE

Imagine receiving airplay and earning income from a song year after year and having that same song be recorded by multiple artists over a span of decades. That is what can happen with a holiday-themed song. For many songwriters and music publishers, landing a holiday recording that becomes the next "White Christmas," "Jingle Bells," or "Rudolph, The Red-Nosed Reindeer," is the greatest gift they could hope for.

While Christmas is likely the first thing that comes to mind when you think about holiday songs, there have been successful songs that relate to other holidays, as well. It would hardly be New Year's Eve without Auld Lang Syne, and there are Valentine's Day songs, songs played on Cinco de Mayo, Chanukah favorites, and St. Patrick's Day songs, such as those recorded by the Irish Rovers and other artists from the Emerald Isle.

There are also songs that are associated with patriotic holidays, and of course, birthday songs.

Michael Jackson's recording of "Thriller" is sure to be heard toward the end of every October, as is "The Time Warp," from the soundtrack of "The Rocky Horror Show." But the song most closely associated with Halloween is the "The Monster Mash" (written by Bobby Pickett and Leonard Capizzi and recorded by Bobby "Boris" Pickett and the Crypt-Kickers). Peaking at #1 when it was released in 1962, the song has charted three subsequent times since its initial release and has been covered by artists including Sha Na Na and the Beach Boys, continuing to generate income for decades.

Trivia buffs might enjoy knowing that legendary songwriter and recording artist Leon Russell played piano on the original recording of "The Monster Mash." Other Halloween perennials include Danny Elfman's "This is Halloween" (from "The Nightmare Before Christmas") and Warren Zevon's "Werewolves of London," (Zevon, Leroy Marinell, Robert Wachtel).

Lee Greenwood's signature song, "God Bless the U.S.A." (written and performed by Greenwood) was first released in 1984, peaking at #7 on Billboard's Hot Country Singles chart. Greenwood's recording of the song was re-released and gained a bigger audience during the Gulf War and following 9/11. The recording charted a second time, reaching #16 on the Billboard Pop chart and #12 on the Adult Contemporary chart, amassing sales of more than one million copies.

American Idol's Season 2 finalists recorded a cover version of "God Bless the U.S.A." that reached #4 on Billboard's Hot 100 chart and was certified "Gold" for selling more than 500,000 copies. Numerous artists, including Beyoncé, have released or performed versions of the song, establishing it as a true holiday standard, and Greenwood's version receives extensive airplay and live performances during every patriotic holiday, such as Veteran's Day, the 4th of July, and Memorial Day, as well as at political rallies. Miley's Cyrus' recording of "Party in the U.S.A." (written by Claude Kelly, Dr. Luke and Jessie J) is likely to receive airplay on the 4th of July and New Year's Eve for many years to come.

Some radio stations alter their formats and play only Christmas music from Thanksgiving through New Year's Day. Billboard magazine lists the popularity of Christmas songs on a U.S. Holiday Song chart. Songs on these playlists can generate royalties for their writers and publishers for a lifetime, but there is a benefit for the recording artists, as well.

Artists who record the first version of a holiday song that becomes a standard ensure that they will receive annual airplay, and remain in the public consciousness for years possibly even decades after their non-holiday releases are no longer included on current playlists. These artists can extend their careers and earn musical immortality by doing annual Christmas concerts and by performing the song closely associated with them on holiday television shows.

Perennial chestnuts such as "Silent Night" and "Deck the Halls" have been part of the Christmas soundtrack for decades, but more recently, songs such as Faith Hill's recording of "Where Are You Christmas," Darlene Love's "Christmas (Baby Please Come Home)," Alabama's "Christmas in Dixie," and Elvis' rendition of "Santa Claus is Back in Town" can be found on Christmas playlists throughout the world.

I spoke with Justin Wilde, owner of Christmas and Holiday Music which is the number one music publisher of original Christmas, Chanukah, Halloween, and other holiday songs. Wilde's company represents more than 240 songwriters and has secured holiday releases with artists including Paul McCartney, Barbra Streisand, Glen Campbell, Anita Baker, Toby Keith, Ray Charles, Loretta Lynn, Johnny Mathis and many more, as well as a long list of television and film placements.

Wilde stated that it has always been difficult to get Christmas and other holiday songs recorded because only a small percentage of releases fall into these categories. Most of the songs on Christmas albums are artists' versions of standards. In some instances, there are no new, original songs included at all. Typically there are not more than two or three original songs included, and with the advent of more artists writing or co-writing the few original songs on their holiday releases, securing these recordings has become even more daunting.

NETFLIX CHRISTMAS MOVIES

Everyone knows that one of the best parts about the holidays is sitting on the couch and watching a good Christmas movie. If you're looking to get into the holiday spirit, there are tons of good flicks streaming on Netflix right now! From comedies to heartfelt romances, we have everything you need to keep yourself entertained. And if you still can't find what you're looking for, check out all the best Christmas streaming on Amazon Prime Video.

BAD SANTA
This 2003 dark comedy starring Billy Bob Thornton has everything adults want in a Christmas movie — humor, profanity, and actually a little bit of heart. It also costars Lauren Graham in what is quite the departure from Lorelai Gilmore.

DEAR SANTA
Who doesn't want to watch Angel and Person of Interest sweetheart Amy Acker learn a valuable holiday lesson as she falls in love with the owner of a soup kitchen? Nobody, that's who. Bonus points: it's directed by Jason Priestley.

GET SANTA
Award-winning actor Jim Broadbent (Iris, Game of Thrones) as Santa Claus who crashes his sleigh and is on the run from the police? Yes, please.

DR. SEUSS' HOW THE GRINCH STOLE CHRISTMAS (2000)
If you can't watch the original cartoon, this Jim Carrey version is the next best thing. He's at his manic best, plus a pre-Gossip Girl Taylor Momsen stars as Cindy Lou Who.

A HOLIDAY ENGAGEMENT
After being unceremoniously dumped, a woman hires a man to play her fiancé for her holiday weekend with the family. Hilarity ensues. Bonnie Somerville, Chris McKenna, Haylie Duff, and Shelley Long are just a few of the "Hey, it's that guy/girl!" faces in this Hallmark charmer.

48 CHRISTMAS WISHES
After a town's letters to Santa get burned, two elves set out to retrieve missing wishes in this film.

holiday Engagement

AS SEEN ON HALLMARK CHANNEL

Hallmark CHANNEL

Now Hiring: A Fiancé for Christmas

CALIFORNIA FIRES:
HOW TO HELP THE VICTIMS OF WOOLSEY FIRE

As the Woolsey and Hill fires burn throughout the greater Los Angeles area, several organizations have boots on the ground and special programs supporting relief efforts. Here's how you can make a difference for those who need it most:

DONATE, VOLUNTEER WITH THE RED CROSS

Those who wish to make cash donations to support Red Cross relief efforts can do so on the Red Cross website or over the phone by calling 1-800-RED-CROSS. You can also text CAWILDFIRES to 90999 to make a $10 donation.

The Red Cross accepts applications for volunteers on its website. Volunteer work ranges from phone calls, data entry and client registration, to shelter support and supply replenishment.

DONATE TO THE VENTURA COUNTY COMMUNITY FOUNDATION

The Ventura County Community Foundation has established the Hill Fire/Woolsey Fire Sudden and Urgent Needs Effort Fund to support the immediate needs of community nonprofit organizations serving those affected by the wildfires.

DONATE TO THE LOS ANGELES FIRE DEPARTMENT FOUNDATION

DONATE CASH OR SUPPLIES TO THE HUMANE SOCIETY OF VENTURA COUNTY

The Humane Society of Ventura County is open for those who have been evacuated and are in need of sanctuary for dogs, cats, horses or other domesticated animals. They said they are in need of 40-gallon horse water troughs and horse electrolytes. Supplies donations can be dropped off at the shelter at 402 Bryant St. in Ojai.

Those who cannot bring supplies to the shelter can make cash donations on HSVC's website.

DONATE TO THE UNITED WAY OF GREATER LOS ANGELES

Those wishing to support the United Way of Greater Los Angeles's wildfire relief efforts can make a cash donation to the organization's Disaster Relief Fund on its website. The organization's relief efforts focus specifically on helping homeless and low-income individuals recover after fires and other natural disasters in the area.

MAKE A CASH DONATION TO THE LOS ANGELES COUNTY ANIMAL CARE FOUNDATION

MAKE A CASH DONATION TO THE LOS ANGELES COUNTY ANIMAL CARE FOUNDATION

The County of Los Angeles Department of Animal Care and Control has opened multiple shelter sites to take in animals displaced by the fires. You can make a cash donation to the Los Angeles County Animal Care Foundation's Noah's Legacy Fund to support the department's disaster relief efforts.

Donations will be used to fund food, shelter and medical care for dogs, cats, horses and other domesticated animals sheltered during a disaster.

DONATE TO THE LOS ANGELES COUNTY FIRE DEPARTMENT FIRE FOUNDATION

The county fire department is helping battle the destructive Woolsey Fire in Los Angeles and Ventura counties.

To donate to the foundation, visit www.lacfdf.org/donate/

DONATE TO THE UNITED WAY OF GREATER LOS ANGELES

Fighting Hunger. Giving Hope.

www.ingramcontent.com/pod-product-compliance
Lightning Source LLC
Chambersburg PA
CBHW060306010526
44108CB00041B/2584